The Love Bear

AF286072

Jenny Jansen

The Love Bear

How the Love Bear got his Name

Bibliographical Information of the ... e Nationalbibliothek

This publication is listed in the D... Nationalbibliographie of the

Deutsche Nationalbibliothek; det... bibliographical information

can be accessed under http: //dnb.d-nb.de

© 2022 Jenny Jansen

Illustrations by Daniela Henninger,

based on ideas and sketches by the author

Cover design, typesetting, production and printing:

BoD — Books on Demand

ISBN 978-3-7568-6431-7

"The Love Bear" was first self-published in 2008, as a debut work. The book is about a boisterous, lively, high-spirited bear cub wearing a red plaid shirt and traditional leather pants. It tells of a bear adventure at Christmas time, of a great mishap and a bearish happy ending. A little "bear teddy" came with the book's first homemade hole binding. The bear cub is now cutting his capers in many new homes.
And from the year 2022 on he wants to bring a lot of joy to my family in the USA. Please, welcome my bear.

Can't you just hear him shouting for joy?

Dedication

This book was born out of the encouragement of the "bear friends" who received the bear as a gift. The little bear is meant to live, to bring joy to all hearts both big and small. The book is dedicated as a thank you to all those who have always believed in me and my little bear friend. A big "2022 bearish" hug for the support to my brother Jesse M., who taught Love Bear many new American words, and to Sandy, who knows the bearish American heartbeat "lub-a-dub".

A very special thank you goes to my husband Joachim, who became a very affectionate "birth assistant" and "father" for the bear cub. Thank you for your courage, the fresh breeze and a big portion of the "going forward" in my life!

My wish is that the little bear, as a Love Bear, makes CHRISTMAS a real celebration of love and friendship for all readers.

MIRACLES are experienced through the LIGHT of HEAVEN in our hearts. Especially at the CHRISTMAS TIME.

Table of Contents

in eight pictures

Introduction

The story

is about a boisterous, lively bear cub
in the exciting Advent season before Christmas,
about an anxious night,
a faithful human child,
a helpful angel
and
a WONDERful
surprise
for Christmas Eve:

"How the Love Bear got his Name".

1. The Boisterous, Lively Bear Cub

There was a big factory in Bear Town. Always at Christmas time, lots of bears were produced. There were lots of beautiful bears on the conveyor belt and one by one they tumbled into a wonderful gift box.

Everywhere, children's hearts were joyfully waiting for their new bear friends. The bear cubs were always full of anticipation about where the journey would take them.

They knew that when the package was opened, a human child would be happy to call such a cuddly and soft bear cub his own.

The bears were excited and wild, wanting to jump into the package right away so that they could quickly make people's hearts beat faster when they reached their new destination.
One of the bear cubs was as boisterous as they come.

"I want to be the first, whoopee!" the cheeky guy shouted exuberantly.

"Whoopee, I'm faster than any of you, I'm the best!"

And so the little bear cub jumped very high and way down the conveyor belt, past all the other bears. And then he jumped mightily one more time.

Bang!
Splat!

12

And then a plop! And there lay the bear cub next to the conveyor belt!
Down below, far away from the other bear cubs, the little bear found himself lying on the floor.
Down among the dirt and the garbage.

Ouch, that hurt! He stretched his bear legs and reached out his bear arms – but what was that?

The bear cub looked down at itself and was shocked. All at once his heart sank. His new bear shirt was torn and hanging down in shreds.

Oh dear, that hurt so much!

But even worse than the problem with the shirt, the bear cub saw a huge hole in his chest. The little bear felt for his heart. Something was missing.
The little bear cub listened and listened, but he couldn't hear a heartbeat.

Where had his heart gotten to?

He no longer felt anything, there was only an empty place where a beating heart had once been.
This made the bear cub very unhappy.

He could hear the other bears laughing and joking up on the conveyor belt. What joy and fun they were having!

But what about him?

He was sitting all alone on the dirty factory floor, with a big hole in his chest and a tattered bear shirt. To his right and left, all he could see was garbage, dirt and soot.

Yuck, he thought, and a big tear rolled out of his left bear's eye. Very slowly it rolled down his cheek. Then he sobbed and cried at the top of his lungs. Can't anyone hear me?

But the others laughed so loudly that no one heard him. Doesn't anyone miss me?

2. The Bear Cub and his Momma

Night fell at the factory, and the conveyor belt was turned off. All the bear cubs were waiting in their cardboard homes for the big wagon that would take them to the children at Christmas.

Only the little bear with the hole in his chest and the torn bear shirt had no home, and was lying all alone under the belt in the dirt.

It was cold and he was very scared. Then he remembered his momma bear.

"Talk to God when you are in trouble, when you are afraid and alone."

That was what she always used to say – back when he was a baby bear, living in the bear home with his brothers and sisters and sometimes got scared and frightened on a dark thunderous stormy night.

He was shaking all over. The factory building was completely dark and all he could hear was his own breathing. He began to stutter, and fearfully tried to bring a sentence past his bear lips. Yes, he wanted to talk to God.

So he sobbed:

> "Dear God, please don't leave me here alone. I really messed up big time. I wanted to be faster and better than the other bear cubs. I wanted to get the biggest bear home and have the most beautiful human child to enjoy me. Please forgive my selfishness, my pride, my wrong behavior. Please do not leave me alone here."

He sighed again, loud and deep. More tears rolled down his cheeks, and then his bear chin sank onto his chest and he fell asleep.

The next morning, he was still lying under the assembly line. That's when he heard footsteps, small but rapid footsteps. He knew them. They belonged to little Mary.

3. Little Mary and the Bear Cub

Mary was the janitor's daughter and always the first to arrive at the factory with her daddy, as they had to clean before dawn.

Mary always collected the scraps of fabric, looked lovingly into each bear box and waved goodbye to them. The little bear waited for Mary with bated breath, hoping she would notice him.

Did she hear him calling?

Mary was sweeping back and forth with her big broom, cleaning up and going about her work. Then her foot bumped into something furry. She stopped working and looked down to the floor.

Oh dear, there was the bear cub lying on the ground! He looked kind of broken, hurt, dented and bent.

"Well now, you poor guy! Little bear, what are you doing here on the ground?" Mary murmured to herself, lost in thought.

She bent down to him. She lovingly picked him up off the floor and cradled him in her arms.

"Oh dear," she exclaimed. "You poor bear cub, what has happened to you? You must have been overdoing it."

"What is up with you?" she asked the little bear cub.
And then she saw what a mess he was in.
She shook her cute black curls with pity.

"Whatever happened here yesterday?" She gently poked his bear nose with her index finger and said tenderly, "Well, probably you were being a bit too boisterous?"

And then she looked at his bear cub body, quite shocked. "What did the bear cub get up to last night?" thought Mary.

The little bear was already ashamed, because he saw at once how she looked at him. She saw the big hole in his chest where he had once had a wonderful strong bear heart, and the rags where he had once been dressed in a fabulous bear shirt.

He would have liked to just disappear. No one should be allowed to see him so dirty and broken.

Mary thought silently, "He can't be wrapped up in a gift box like that anymore. He won't be allowed to go on a trip now."

But she had already come to a decision. "I'm not going to send him to the trash and dump him with the scraps of cloth I collected!"

Mary thought about it, and then she had a great idea.

Mary took the little bear cub and put him on a shelf. She was going to get him a new bear shirt, if she had time, and somehow plug the hole in his bear chest. That was all she could do for him now.

She lovingly stroked his bear head again and said that she would stop by again in the evening and help him. All she could do for now was save him from final destruction, from being thrown away in the trash.

So our boisterous little bear sat on the shelf, and with a heavy heart had to look on all day as the other bear cubs joyfully moved to their new homes. How he regretted his high spirits now!

Had his prayer helped just a bit?

He had really hoped that God would help him. Hadn't he been talking to God all night?

In the evening it became dark again in the factory and the bear cub wondered why Mary didn't come. "She must have forgotten about me," thought the little bear cub. Oh dear, yet another night was ahead of him.

But the little bear began to be grateful that he had not been thrown into the garbage, but at least had been given a place on the shelf. The bear cub was sad, because he wanted so much to be with the human children, and now he was just lying here on the shelf. He sobbed.

He was rescued, but broken and tattered. Tears rolled down his bear cub cheeks again.

If only he had listened to his mother. What had his exuberance led him into?

He thought to himself that he would just talk to God again and then ask not only to be saved, but also for a new bear shirt and, above all, for a new bear heart.

He felt abandoned by Mary. So the second night he sobbed to himself:

"Please, dear God, give me a new bear heart according to Your will and please give me" – he took a deep breath – "a new bear shirt, as well."

Then he fell asleep, completely exhausted.

4. The Angel and the Bear Cub

A hand touched him gently. The bear cub first opened his right eye, and then, very slowly and tentatively, he opened his left eyelid as well.

What was going on?

The little bear cub had fallen asleep. Who was waking him up?

Had Mary come back?

But no, he saw a wonderful lady with long blond curls who began to address him in gentle tones:

"Fear not, little bear. God has heard your prayers.
God has heard you apologize for your behavior and
repent for what you have done.
HE has sent me so that you will not be alone
tonight. Do not be afraid anymore.
I am an angel sent by God especially for you."

The bear cub felt a warm gentle breeze, and he felt quite warm as well, there in the place where once his heart had been – where the big hole in his chest was now.

The bear cub felt it was a very special moment. He could not get enough of the beauty of the angel. Then, very quietly, he dared to ask:

"So when will I get my new heart and, … and shirt?"

The angel laughed and gently stroked his bear shoulders.

"You boisterous little bear, I guess you can't wait. Have patience. Aren't you glad that I'm here, that God has personally assigned me to watch over YOU? God is walking with you step by step and bit by bit. All in His good time. I do not know the hour when you will be made completely new."

"All right," the bear cub thought to himself, "I will try to be patient, and now that my angel is here, I will try to go back to sleep. I am resting in God's hand."

The next morning the little bear woke up, and he knew something had happened during the night. He thought he had been dreaming.

But then Mary came, just like every morning, and shouted with joy:
"Little bear cub, I've got your new shirt!"

Then she stopped in mid-sentence: "But you already have a new shirt. What a beautiful garment! Who gave it to you?" Mary almost did a somersault.

Only now did the little bear notice that he had a new shirt on. No more rags, everything was much nicer than the shirt he had before.

Then he remembered his prayer and the conversation with the angel the previous night.

He told Mary everything, and knew he had not been dreaming.
God had helped him. Yes, an angel had actually spoken to him and comforted him.

But Mary still seemed sad. She knew he didn't have a new heart yet. There was still a hole there in his chest.

And a heart is more important than a shirt, she thought. Even though he was now dressed in a new bear shirt, he still had a hole in the place of the rib cage, in the place where the bear cub had once heard his bear heart beating.

The wild little bear thought to himself that now he had survived two nights already and had been saved from being thrown away in the garbage.

God Himself had sent him an angel and he had already been given a new bear shirt. But how he wanted to hear his heart beat again! How he missed hearing his heart jumping!
And now that Mary was with him, he really took courage again and said to himself, "I'm praying again tonight! Everything will be all right again."

The angel had explained to him that his time as a bear was in God's hands. Mary had also become quite curious as to how everything would continue. Secretly, she admired the strong little bear. It seemed that somehow or other he was growing up.

She squeezed him and gave him a little kiss on his soft bear cheek.

"Well, just wait till tomorrow and then we'll see."

As she left, Mary thought about Christmas and that tomorrow was already "Holy Night" (that's what mankind call the night before Christmas).

No, the bear cub would not have had a chance to be packed into the gift box for a human child, when all he had was a hole in the place of a heart.

Human children want heart-full bears, not heart-less bear cubs. Human children want bears to be cuddly.

Mary wanted to help the little bear cub, and thought of bringing a needle and thread and sewing up the bear cub's wound on the morning of Christmas Eve. At least then he would no longer have a hole in his bear cub chest, she thought.

But how could she replace his missing heart?

Would it help him if she took him home and loved him a lot? Or if she gave him a really great cuddle?

Would the bear cub then grow a heart again in the place of the hole?

Mary shook her black curls back and forth. She felt uncertain. She went back to our bear cub for a moment and explained:

"Dear little bear cub, I'm going to ask my daddy to help us. I have taken you into my heart and I want to help you. Don't give up, I'll think of a way!" she called out to him, and blew him a kiss as she walked off.

The bear cub saw her skipping out of the bear workshop, and fell asleep reassured. Mary would help him, he could rely on her. The little bear cub realized that Mary had already become very fond of him.

Full of anticipation, the bear cub looked forward to the new day, which was to be Christmas Eve. What surprises would this special day, this special evening hold for the little bear?

5. The Bear Cub's Dream

In the night our bear cub dreamed again.
The little bear cub was holding God's hand and walking through a beautiful colorful bear garden. It smelled of roses.

The stars shone and paved the way for them.

God Himself stroked him on the shoulder and said:

> "I am with you all the days of your life. Do not be afraid. Be happy. I carry you. As soon as tomorrow you will see the miracle I have worked."

The bear cub leapt for joy in the dream and he felt whole and well. Yes, this garden was so wonderful and the little bear cub was able to be with God. The bear cub was so happy that he didn't even want to wake up.

Someone called his name:

"Good morning, bear cub, it's Christmas already! Are you awake yet? How did you sleep? Hello, it's Mary, wake up!"

He felt a gentle shaking of his bear's shoulders and something tickled his ear. Mary's voice was very close now and he felt her breathing on his little bear's ear.

The little bear cub opened his left eye and still blinked quite sleepily with his right.

"Mmm, do I have to wake up already?" he mumbled. "I was having such a beautiful dream." The bear cub sighed – he didn't much want to wake up and face reality.

But God had a wonderful plan for the bear cub that Christmas morning. The little bear cub was a very special bear cub to Him. And God's plans are always good. Little Mary was a part of His wonderful plan for the bear cub.

And so Mary took the bear cub off the shelf, and when she looked at the little bear, she was startled.

"Bear cub, bear cub!" she cried. "I've brought needle and thread. I want to darn your hole and sew it up. But..."

Mary stood there with her mouth open and her eyes wide: "There's no hole at all anymore!"

6. How the Bear Cub got his Name

"Little bear, what happened last night?" she asked in amazement.

The bear cub had not yet realized what had happened to him overnight. He told her about his dream in which God had taken him for a walk.

Lovingly, Mary stroked the little bear. Her hand slid over his bear shirt, and there she felt something unusual. It crackled like paper. She felt it a bit more closely and there was a small piece of paper in her hand. The paper was filled with a beautiful script.

"Bear cub, there's a note!" she exclaimed loudly, and pulled it out of his bear shirt pocket.

This was the message on the paper, written by the hand of God:

"Bear cub, from this day forth, you bear my name.
You have received a brand new sparkling heart
from Me. It is different from your first heart.
I have given you a yellow heart.
Your heart will shine as brightly as the sun.

I Myself have closed the seam of your wounds with
the invisible thread of forgiving love, and included
healing for your soul with every stitch.

No scars will remain visible. What is done by ME is perfect and complete.

When you enter a human house, the human children will rejoice in your sunny yellow bear's heart, and the happiness of My blessing will come to them through you. Whoever holds you in his arms will feel God's love.

Little bear cub, I give you a new name: You are my Love Bear."

You are
my
"Love Bear"

Only now did the bear cub realize that he had been holding his breath the whole time Mary had been reading.

Now, finally, the little bear dared to take a deep breath. The bear cub looked at Mary with his deep black eyes and was almost speechless.

Yes, the angel had told him: God Himself had gone for a walk with him and had answered his pleading prayers.

Then he noticed that his bear body felt all warm again, and he felt the life inside him.

He looked at his bear chest and there was no more hole, no more tatters.

The little bear was amazed and wept for joy.

"Lub-dub, lub-dub, lub-a-dub, thump, thump!" his heart went, and he felt his heart really leaping.

"Thump, thump, hippity hop!" it went inside him, and with his bear voice he began to thank God aloud with a bear song.

His prayers had been answered by God personally. He had been given a new heart. And a new heartbeat tone forever. Not just any old heart, but a very, very special yellow sun heart, and even a new bear shirt as well.

Now he could believe in Christmas after all.

Yes, he could still go on his journey and finally be allowed to move in with human children as a "love bear" he was meant to be.

Can't you just hear the jubilation?

7. The Love Bear Dances with his Mary

Mary took the bear cub in her arms, and they danced around the factory floor with joy at his having been healed.

All the gift boxes had already been packed and the big trucks were already on their way to the human children, so Mary got to keep the bear cub for herself that Christmas Eve.

That Christmas Eve, these Christmas Days the little bear cub brightened Mary's little world with his new sunny golden yellow heart.

He brought so much light and brightness into the janitor's apartment that Mary's parents said:

> "We don't really need any candles on the Christmas tree today.
> Mary, you and your Love Bear shine with happiness brighter than a thousand stars in the firmament heavens."

Mary hugged her Love Bear tightly and tenderly to her heart and kissed him.

8. The Love Bear celebrates Christmas

"I love you so much," Mary whispered into his bear's ear – and you know what?

The Love Bear got quite red in the face, because he was so happy.

Yes, he had found his place. And he was no longer alone on the shelf. But the best thing of all was that it was Christmas.

This Christmas, however, the bear cub chosen by God and named "Love Bear" brought Mary such love and joy as can only be given by God.

And now guess who else was happy about that the bear cub was with?

Mary's Mom and Dad became happy again, because they felt the kindness and goodness of the Love Bear flowing into their hearts as well.

And what happened after Christmas?

What will happen next with the Love Bear and little Mary?

To be continued...

For the Love Bear had no idea that his sunny yellow heart held a great secret. God is so good. HE has a special plan for our bear cub.

And if you want to know all the wonderful things that happened to the Love Bear, we all can read about it in the next book:

"The Love Bear
and His Secret"

About the Author

Jenny Jansen grew up as an adopted child in the Catholic parsonage "Kirmutscheid" located in Germany, named "The Eifel – Region" in the municipality of Adenau.

Her favorite place there was the old parsonage village library. Books became her best friends. A natural, rural environment gave her a colorful childhood. Trees and flowers wove stories into her heart.

Her life's journey led her via a commercial apprenticeship and evening classes into the world of banking and insurance. But people and their questions, worries and needs have remained her main concern to this day.

A serious illness led to an unintended "forced rest" from the exhausting daily job routine. The only one who listened to her stories was her teddy bear – a gift from her friend Rosemarie Uschold. He was supposed to comfort her and love her. And then something amazing happened! During one of her many sleepless nights in Advent 2007, the "Love Bear" asked to be brought to life, and has accompanied the author ever since that winter as a firm friend, one who gets to experience many adventures in her stories.

Meanwhile as a consultant, speaker and trained systemic business coach, she supports people in the most diverse areas of their lives.